History for Kids: The Illustrated Lives of Founding Fathers - George Washington, Thomas Jefferson, Benjamin Franklin, Alexander Hamilton, and James Madison

By Charles River Editors

About Charles River Editors

Charles River Editors was founded by Harvard and MIT alumni to provide superior editing and original writing services, with the expertise to create digital content for publishers across a vast range of subject matter. In addition to providing original digital content for third party publishers, Charles River Editors republishes civilization's greatest literary works, bringing them to a new generation via ebooks.

Sign up here to receive updates about free books as we publish them, and visit Our Kindle Author Page to browse today's free promotions and our most recently published Kindle titles.

Introduction

Benjamin Franklin (1755-1835)

Before the United States of America even existed, the first American celebrity was Benjamin Franklin (1706-1790). In his career, Franklin was an author, printer, political theorist, politician, postmaster, scientist, musician, inventor, satirist, civic activist, statesman, and diplomat. After having his hand in all kinds of community service in Philadelphia, and inventing important devices like lightning rods, Franklin used his unique status as an international celebrity to become the colonies' best diplomat, first as an ambassador to Britain and then as an ambassador to France during the American Revolution. Franklin was particularly revered in Enlightened France, where he skillfully negotiated French entry into the Revolutionary War in a manner that practically bankrupted them, a critical step that helped the colonists win their independence. After negotiating the Treaty of Paris, Franklin played a role at the Constitutional Convention in his adopted home town of Philadelphia during the twilight of his life.

Like other Founding Fathers, Franklin's lengthy career and magnificent exploits have been heavily embellished, to the point that some of the myths of Franklin's life are better known than the man himself. In addition to highlighting his life and legacy, this book also humanizes the First American. Along with pictures of Franklin and other important people and events in his life, your kids will learn about Franklin like they never have before.

George Washington (1732-1799)

Every American is taught a pristine narrative of the life and legacy of George Washington and can easily recite the highlights of the "Father of Our Country". The remarkable Virginian led an under-resourced rag-tag army to ultimate victory in the American Revolution before becoming the nation's first president, setting it on its path toward superpower status. He may not have actually chopped down a cherry tree or tossed a silver dollar across the Potomac, but his contemporaries considered his character above reproach.

When Washington voluntary resigned as commander of the armies, he stunned the world. Everyone in the colonies and the world realized that Washington, at the head of the last army standing in the colonies, could have made himself king of the new United States on the spot, and it would have been a move supported by his rank and file soldiers. Instead, Washington became the first Westerner to voluntarily demobilize his army, ensuring civilian control of the new nation. King George III called Washington "the greatest character of the age" for making that decision.

As President from 1788-1796, Washington set every precedent for the executive branch of the new government, from forming a "Cabinet" to limiting himself to two terms. He even set precedents with his farewell address, which helped guide the policies of subsequent presidents.

Washington did more than any other man to ensure the success of the American Revolution and the safe passage of the new United States from fledgling nation to budding power, but what actually made the man tick? Underneath his steel surface burned an almost insatiable political ambition, and a man who was acutely self-conscious of himself. In addition to highlighting his life and legacy, this book humanizes the leader who is now remembered more like a flawless demigod than a man. Along with pictures of the Father of Our Country and other important people and events in his life, your kids will learn about Washington like never before.

Thomas Jefferson (1743-1826)

The story of the United States of America is one of a nation founded upon the loftiest ideals of representative government, attempting to fulfill its goals while encountering competing domestic and global forces. From the beginning, Americans debated how their national government should govern, balancing powers between the federal government and the states, which led to the establishment of the first political parties. At the same time, the nation has struggled to reconcile its guarantee of universal rights and individual liberties with several stark realities, including the presence of millions of slaves at the time of the Declaration of Independence.

Nobody spent more time in the thick of these debates than **Thomas Jefferson**, one of the most famous and revered Americans. Jefferson was instrumental in all of the aforementioned debates, authoring the Declaration of Independence, laying out the ideological groundwork of the notion of states' rights, leading one of the first political parties, and overseeing the expansion of the United States during his presidency.

But for all of his accomplishments, Jefferson's reputation and legacy are still inextricably intertwined with the divisive issues of his own day. As the slaveholder who wrote that all men are created equal, and his relationship with one of his slaves, Sally Hemings, Jefferson's life and career are still sometimes fiercely debated today.

This book discusses these accomplishments, while also humanizing the leader whose words literally created a new nation, and whose hand guided the political debates and Manifest Destiny of the nation he helped create. Along with pictures of this Founding Father and other important people and events in his life, your kids will learn about Jefferson like never before.

James Madison (1751-1836)

In Charles River Editors' History for Kids series, your children can learn about history's most important people and events in an easy, entertaining, and educational way. Pictures help bring the story to life, and the concise but comprehensive book will keep your kid's attention all the way to the end.

The Founding Fathers have become so revered by Americans in the last 200 years that the "Father of the Constitution" himself is often overlooked among the rest of the pantheon. Today James Madison's legacy mostly pales in comparison to the likes of George Washington, Ben Franklin and his closest colleague, Thomas Jefferson, but Madison's list of important accomplishments is monumental.

A lifelong statesman, Madison was the youngest delegate at the Continental Congress from 1780-83, and at 36 he was one of the youngest men who headed to Philadelphia for the Constitutional Convention in 1787. Despite his age, he was the Convention's most influential thinker, and the man most responsible for the final draft of the U.S. Constitution. Along with Alexander Hamilton and John Jay, Madison was one of the most persuasive advocates for ratifying the Constitution, authoring some of the most famous Federalist Papers, and he drafted the Bill of Rights that was later added to the Constitution.

Even after that, Madison's work was far from done. Along with Thomas Jefferson, Madison was one of the founders and ideological cornerstones of the Democratic-Republican Party that guided the young nation in the first 30 years of the 19th century. That included his own presidency, during which he oversaw the War of 1812.

Like the other Founding Fathers, Madison is better known in word and deed than as an actual person. This book covers Madison's incredible accomplishments, but it also humanizes the classic thinker who idolized Thomas Jefferson and had a loving relationship with wife Dolley, who helped mold the position of First Lady as debutante. Along with pictures of Madison and other important people and events in his life, your kids will learn about the Father of the Constitution like never before.

Alexander Hamilton (circa 1755-1804)

In Charles River Editors' History for Kids series, your children can learn about history's most important people and events in an easy, entertaining, and educational way. Pictures help bring the story to life, and the concise but comprehensive book will keep your kid's attention all the way to the end.

The Founding Fathers have been revered by Americans for over 200 years, celebrated for creating a new nation founded upon the loftiest ideals of democracy and meritocracy. But if the American Dream has come to represent the ability to climb the social ladder with skill and hard work, no Founding Father represented the new America more than Alexander Hamilton.

Unfortunately, one of the best known aspects of Hamilton's (1755-1804) life is the manner in which he died, shot and killed in a famous duel with Aaron Burr in 1804. But Hamilton started as an orphaned child in the West Indies before becoming one of the most instrumental Founding Fathers of the United States in that time, not only in helping draft and gain support for the U.S. Constitution but in also leading the Federalist party and building the institutions of the young federal government as Washington's Secretary of Treasury.

Hamilton is also well remembered for his authorship, along with John Jay and James Madison, of the *Federalist Papers*. The *Federalist Papers* sought to rally support for the Constitution's approval when those three anonymously wrote them, but they demonstrate how men of vastly different political ideologies came to accept the same Constitution.

Like the other American Legends, much of Hamilton's personal life has been overshadowed by the momentous events in which he participated, from the Revolutionary War to the most famous duel in American history. This book covers the amazing and various facets of Hamilton's life and career, putting a human touch on the man who gave as good as he got, but always put what he felt were the country's interests ahead of his own political interests. Along with pictures of Hamilton and other important people and events in his life, your kids will learn about this essential Founding Father like never before.

History for Kids: The Illustrated Lives of Founding Fathers - George Washington, Thomas Jefferson, Benjamin Franklin, Alexander Hamilton, and James Madison

About Charles River Editors

Introduction

Benjamin Franklin

   Chapter 1: Young Benjamin Franklin

   Chapter 2: Writing and Publishing

   Chapter 3: A Public Figure

   Chapter 4: Britain and the Colonies Get Mad

   Chapter 5: The American Revolution

   Chapter 6: The Constitutional Convention of 1787

   Chapter 7: Franklin's Final Years

George Washington

   Chapter 1: Washington's Early Life and Education, 1732 – 1753

   Chapter 2: The French & Indian War

   Chapter 3: Trouble with Britain

   Chapter 4: The American Revolution

   Chapter 5: The Constitutional Convention of 1787

   Chapter 6: President Washington

   Chapter 7: The Father of Our Country

   True or False?

Thomas Jefferson

   Chapter 1: Early Life

   Chapter 2: The American Revolution

   Chapter 3: Serving His Country

   Chapter 4: President George Washington

   Chapter 5: President Jefferson

   Chapter 6: Final Years

James Madison

   Chapter 1: Early Years

   Chapter 2: The American Revolution

   Chapter 3: The Father of the Constitution

   Chapter 4: Early American Government

   Chapter 5: President Madison

   Chapter 6: Madison's Last Years

Alexander Hamilton
- Chapter 1: An Orphan
- Chapter 2: The Revolutionary War
- Chapter 3: The Constitution
- Chapter 4: Secretary of the Treasury
- Chapter 5: A New Job
- Chapter 6: The Hamilton-Burr Duel

Benjamin Franklin

Chapter 1: Young Benjamin Franklin

Benjamin Franklin was born here in Boston

On January 17th, 1706, Josiah Franklin's 15th child was born. He named his new son Benjamin. Benjamin would grow up in a family of 17 children.

Benjamin lived in Boston. Franklin's childhood days were spent playing by the Charles River. The Charles River was very close to his home in Boston. The family's two room home was not big enough to play in, so he had to play somewhere else.

At the age of 6, Benjamin's family moved into a bigger home. That year, the last Franklin child was born. She was Benjamin's sister, Jane. Benjamin liked Jane more than anybody else.

Benjamin's dad wanted Benjamin to be a priest. Benjamin wrote, "I was put to the grammar-school at eight years of age, my father intending to devote me, as the tithe of his sons, to the service of the Church."

Benjamin was good at reading. He would later write that he could not remember a time when he couldn't read! When he was 8, Benjamin was sent to the Boston Latin School. Benjamin did well at Boston Latin. Benjamin's dad wanted him to go to Harvard. There he could learn to be a great minister. One of the first books Franklin read was *Pilgrim's Progress*. It was written by a religious Puritan named John Bunyan.

Benjamin was very smart, but he didn't do very well in school. When he went to writing and arithmetic school, Benjamin failed arithmetic. Benjamin had to leave school, but he also found out he was good at writing.

Benjamin's parents did not have the money for him to go to Harvard. Benjamin was only 10 when he stopped going to school.

Benjamin Franklin's parents have a big grave in Boston. It is in the Granary Burying Ground in Boston, a mile away from where Benjamin was born. John Hancock, Samuel Adams, and Paul Revere are also buried there!

When he was still a young boy, Benjamin went to work in his father's candle and soap shop. Benjamin didn't like working in his father's shop. He would later write that his father's trade was dying. He "was employed in cutting wick for the candles, filling the dipping mold and the molds for cast candles, attending the shop, going of errands, etc."

Benjamin said the work was boring and no fun. His father's shop was always filled with bad smells. Benjamin was simply not cut out for making soap and candles.

Instead, Benjamin decided to go to sea. He learned how to swim at an early age. He also learned how to sail on boats with other boys in the town. Benjamin's dad didn't like that his son played in the water. His dad made him do something else. Benjamin found a new job he liked:

printing. His brother James had traveled to England to learn how to set up a print shop.

At the age of 12, Benjamin became a printer in his brother's shop. He was supposed to work there for 9 years. Franklin was happy there, but he didn't want to stay until he was 21. Benjamin asked if he could only have to stay for 7 years. His brother said no.

Working as a printer was a natural job for Benjamin. He already spent all the money he could on books. In 1721, his brother James founded a newspaper in Boston. It was called the *New England Courant*. When Benjamin was just 15, the *New England Courant* published his first written work. James was never aware of the essays Benjamin wrote.

Benjamin sent essays under the nickname "Silence Dogood." They were very funny. Benjamin pretended to be an old widowed woman. The articles were very popular. This left many people guessing who was writing them.

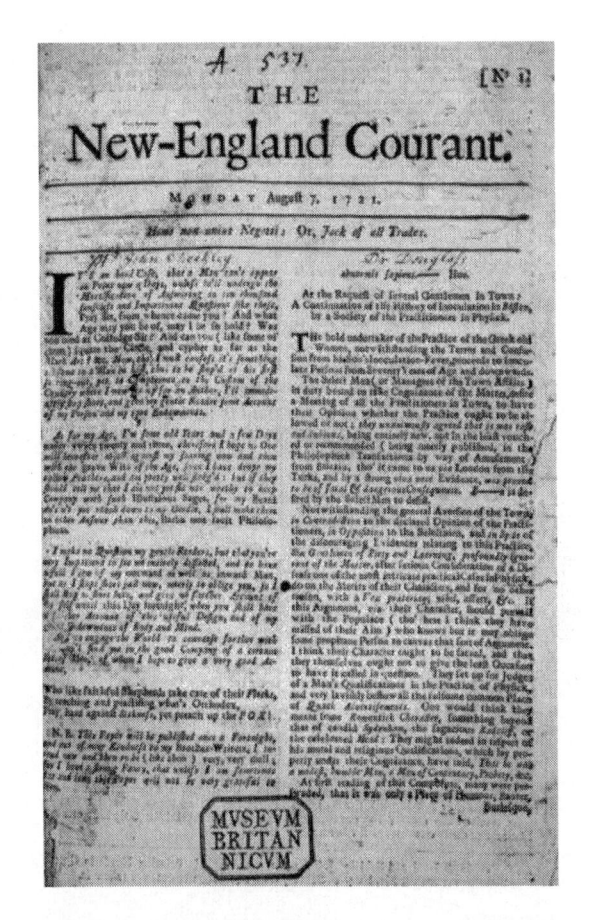

The first issue of the *New England Courant*, dated 1721

Chapter 2: Writing and Publishing

Silence Dogood was popular. However, the colony was still influenced by the Puritans. The articles made the Puritans angry. The paper poked fun at the city's Puritan ethics. Many religious leaders took offense. They took legal action against the paper. James Franklin was banned from publishing the *Courant*.

James had another plan. He realized that his ban did not mean the paper had to be stopped.

He decided to pretend to pass control of the paper over to Benjamin. But he would still control things behind the scenes. To do that, James said Benjamin would no longer have to be an apprentice for 9 years. Then he made Benjamin the publisher. But James did force his younger brother to sign a secret agreement to remain an apprentice.

A painting of Benjamin working in the printing press

Benjamin felt this was wrong. If he was the paper's publisher, why did he need more training? He decided that it was time to start elsewhere. He no longer wanted to go to sea. Instead, he decided to run away to Philadelphia. He was 17 years old.

In Philadelphia, Benjamin met many new people. He used his skills in printing to get his first job. He worked for a man named Samuel Keimer. Keimer was one of Philadelphia's only printers. He was also rather odd. The two got along well. They even discussed starting a new religion!

Franklin talked with many of Keimer's customers. One of them was Sir William Keith, the governor of Pennsylvania. Governor Keith was unhappy with the printing being done in his colony. He hoped to bring better services to the colony. He saw a great future for Benjamin. He offered to pay Benjamin to sail to London. He wanted him to learn printing first hand.

Benjamin left for London in November 1724. On the way, he met a man named Thomas

Denham. In London, Franklin learned typesetting and bought some printing equipment. Still, he missed Philadelphia. Philadelphia was truly his home. In 1726, he and his new friend returned to Pennsylvania. They opened a shop together.

Sadly, Benjamin's friend died just after they opened the shop. He was forced to close his shop, so he returned to Keimer's for a short time. But Benjamin was good at networking. He had friends across the city.

In 1729, Franklin and some of his friends formed the Leather Apron Club. This became known as the "Junto." Junto was for smart people. The people in the club talked about the issues of the day. They also passed around information.

During this time, Franklin married Deborah Read. He had met her when he first moved to Philadelphia years earlier. Then his proposal to her was rejected. Read's family thought Benjamin did not have enough money. By 1730, Benjamin had enough money. Deborah's family consented to the marriage. .

Deborah Read

Franklin was becoming a very important person in Philadelphia. A year before his marriage, he made the *Pennsylvania Gazette*. It soon became a good newspaper. In 1731, Franklin founded the Philadelphia Library. His friends from the Junto helped him.

The library began as a compilation of the group's private books. It collected more and more books. In 1739, the library moved to the building that housed the Pennsylvania State House. This made it an important place in the city of Philadelphia.

The frame marks the location of Benjamin Franklin's house in Philadelphia

Chapter 3: A Public Figure

In 1732, Franklin began publishing *Poor Richard's Almanack.* He wasn't doing it as a writing outlet. He was being practical. He needed money. Franklin didn't hide this. He wrote "the plain truth of the matter is, I am excessive poor, and my wife…has threatened more than once to burn all my books and Rattling-Traps if I do not make some profitable use of them for the good of my family."

An almanac gave people advice, weather forecasts and amusing puzzles. *Poor Richard's* is best known for its sayings. One of these was "early to bed, early to rise, makes a young man healthy, wealthy and wise." Each book encouraged saving money.

The almanac was published from 1732 to 1758. It made Benjamin a lot of money. It is still the most famous American almanac in history.

Franklin liked to help everyone in Philadelphia. In 1736, he made the Union Fire Company. It was the first volunteer firefighting company in North America. He was able to do this because of his position as Clerk of the General Assembly.

Franklin continued to study and get smarter. He began to study languages. He learned French, Italian, Spanish and Latin. He also joined the Freemasons. He became the Philadelphia lodge's Grand Master in 1734.

In 1739, the famed minister George Whitefield came to Philadelphia. Franklin was not really a Christian. Still, he enjoyed discussing ideas, so he decided to meet with Whitefield. The two struck a deal for Franklin to publish his sermons.

George Whitefield

Benjamin became a very important inventor. He created a lot of new things. His first big invention was the Franklin Stove in 1741. It was a wood-burning stove that could be built into fireplaces. This would produce more heat with less smoke and drafts.

A Franklin Stove

In 1743, Franklin founded the American Philosophical Society. It was a place to discuss scientific theories. Franklin then became interested in electricity. He soon gathered the materials he needed to study electricity.

Benjamin didn't think electricity was created by friction. He thought it was collected by friction. This helped him learn about positive and negative charges. Franklin thought that electricity and lightning were similar. He thought that lightning might be a form of electricity. But he needed a way of be sure. He tried an experiment. He flew a kite with a key attached during a thunderstorm. He got electrical sparks from a cloud.

This led Benjamin to invent the lightning rod. It would capture lightning from the sky. It would also keep it from starting fires on buildings. He also invented the bifocal lens. These help people see better.

Franklin's inventions made him famous in the 13 colonies and in Europe.

In 1743, Franklin wanted to make a new school in Philadelphia. By 1749, his new school became the University of Pennsylvania. In 1751, Franklin helped make Pennsylvania Hospital. It was the first hospital in America. Franklin started organizations to teach his fellow citizens.

A drawing of Pennsylvania Hospital

In 1750, Franklin started working in Pennsylvania General Assembly. He served there for 14 years. While he was there, he met with Indians. These Indians wanted to get support from the colonists. It didn't work.

The British then made Franklin the Deputy Postmaster for the Colonies. This was the best postal job in America. He held this post until 1774.

In 1754, a bigger reward came to Franklin. He was chosen for the Albany Colonial Congress. It wanted to support unity in the 13 colonies. Franklin had big ideas for colonial unity. He was happy to attend the meeting.

Franklin proposed a plan to unite the colonies under a single government. It proved to be a guide for the later Constitution of the United States.

In 1756, the colonies and England were at war with France. Franklin joined the war as a Colonel. He had earlier tried to make an all-volunteer militia. This made the Quakers happy that they did not have to join. Benjamin spent very little time in the war and didn't fight very much.

In 1757, the colonies decided to send Franklin to London, England. They hoped the British would like him. They thought he would be the most popular person to talk to the British.

Benjamin arrived in London to help the colonies. Benjamin toured England and met a lot of new friends. But the British were unhappy with the colonies in the 1760s. This is when troubles with the 13 colonies began. Benjamin was in London for five years, and he became unhappy with the British. The British did not respect the colonies.

1759 portrait of Franklin

Chapter 4: Britain and the Colonies Get Mad

In September, 1761, Franklin watched King George III being crowned. He still liked the British. He hoped the king would be nicer to the American colonies.

King George III

   Franklin decided to return to the colonies. His time at home was different than before he left for London. He spent much of 1763 checking out the postal offices in the northern colonies. He was looking for ways to make them better.

   In 1763, a new Governor came to Pennsylvania. His name was John Penn. He was someone Franklin met at the Albany Conference. He thought Penn would be different.

   In 1763, France and Britain stopped fighting, but there were still a lot of Indians in Pennsylvania. A group called the Paxton Boys did not like this. They decided to kill Indians living in Pennsylvania.

   When they killed Indians, it made Franklin very mad. The Indians were peaceful Christians who never fought them. But then the Paxtons marched towards Philadelphia. They wanted to kill Indians there too. Franklin wanted the Governor to use militia to stop the Paxtons.

   The Governor made a truce with the Paxtons. They agreed to not kill Indians in Philadelphia.

But the governor did not punish the Paxtons. He offered money for the Paxtons to kill Indians elsewhere. This made Franklin so mad that he made a group to force the governor to lose his next election.

Pennsylvania sent Franklin back to England to talk to the British. He went to London in early 1765. In 1765, the British Parliament began to pass new taxes on the 13 colonies. Many believed that Parliament had no right to raise taxes. Parliament had no American members. The colonists argued that they could not raise taxes on them. The new tax acts began in 1765 with the Stamp Act. The Stamp Act said that paper used for printing must carry a valid stamp. This would show that a tax had been paid to the British.

The Stamp Act was the first tax that Parliament passed. It was repealed in 1766. Then Parliament passed an act giving itself the power to tax the colonies. This angered the colonists who just fought the Stamp Act.

The tax acts continued in 1767. The Revenue Act of 1767 taxed items that came to the colonies. Americans did not like the Revenue Act either.

Parliament passed the Quartering Act of 1765. It forced people in the colonies to let British soldiers live in their houses. The soldiers could stay for free in inns, barns or public houses. Parliament assumed that the colonies would build places for the troops. That did not happen.

Franklin talked to the British on behalf of the colonies. But the British would not treat him well. In 1766, several colonies chose Franklin as their representative in London. Franklin's dream of unity was coming true.

Then Franklin made a mistake. He suggested a friend be a stamp collector in the colonies. Colonists thought he was supporting the Stamp Act. Benjamin began writing letters in support of a boycott. He also asked Parliament to get rid of the Stamp Act.

The Stamp Act was repealed in 1766. However, more taxes were coming. The Townshend Acts were a series of laws passed beginning in 1767. They made the colonists mad. This surprised Franklin. He did not think they were that bad. Now both the colonists and the British were mad at him. Franklin kept working for the colonists though. They started to like him again.

Painting of Benjamin Franklin in 1767

Chapter 5: The American Revolution

The British made the colonists very angry in 1774. They passed more acts because of the Boston Tea Party. The British Parliament passed a series of acts to punish Boston and the colony of Massachusetts. They closed Boston's harbor. Parliament hoped to force the colonies to obey them. Instead, colonists were even angrier. Many colonists viewed the acts as a violation of their rights. In 1774, they organized the First Continental Congress. It met in Philadelphia to coordinate a protest.

The Congress declared that they had rights. They also talked about a boycott on the British. The First Continental Congress asked the British government to end the bad acts. They also agreed to meet again next summer.

Benjamin decided to return home in 1775. He set out for another journey across the ocean. He arrived in Philadelphia on May 5th, 1775.

Massachusetts was a problem for Britain. It began with the Boston Massacre in 1770. Then came the Boston Tea Party in December 1773. After this, the British put a military command in place over Boston.

In early 1775, General Thomas Gage heard that colonists had weapons in Concord, Massachusetts. Gage sent 700 British soldiers to take the weapons. Patriot leaders heard about this. Men warned the people of Lexington and Concord the night before.

General Gage

The local militia met the British soldiers at Lexington. Shots were fired and some colonists were killed. The British soldiers marched to Concord. There they met more armed colonists. Colonists came from other places to fight the British as they marched back to Boston. Many British soldiers died trying to get back to Boston. The American Revolution had begun.

The pleas of the First Continental Congress had no effect on King George III or Parliament. The Second Continental Congress decided to convene in June, 1775. By then, colonists had taken things into their own hands. The First Continental Congress had met for 6 months. The Second Continental Congress would last for 6 years.

People were happy when Franklin came home. They chose him to be part of the Second Continental Congress. Then he became Postmaster General in July 1775. He was now 70 years old, the oldest person in the Congress. But he was much respected.

Franklin told the other members of Congress that they should make the "Articles of Confederation and Perpetual Union." It would help the colonists rule the colonies without Britain. The Articles of Confederation were created in 1776.

On June 17, 1775, the bloodiest battle of the whole Revolution would be fought. It happened at Bunker Hill, across the Charles River from Boston. The Battle of Bunker Hill helped make the colonial soldiers feel better about themselves. They continued to surround Boston and trap the British there.

Some delegates tried to think of ways the colonies could get along with the Britain. Soon they began to think independence was best. The Congress chose 5 men to write a document explaining why they wanted independence. Benjamin Franklin, John Adams, and Thomas Jefferson were 3 of the 5 men. Everyone agreed that Jefferson should write it.

Thomas Jefferson

After Jefferson wrote a draft, Franklin read it and made changes. He did not like Jefferson's line "we hold these truths to be sacred and undeniable." He changed it to "we hold these truths to be self-evident." Jefferson listened to Franklin and rewrote it. It is now the most famous part of the Declaration of Independence:

"We hold these truths to be self-evident, that all men are created equal, that they are endowed by their Creator with certain unalienable Rights, that among these are Life, Liberty and the pursuit of Happiness."

Painting of the 5 men showing a draft of the Declaration of Independence.

After the Declaration of Independence, the colonies needed to find other people to help them fight. They wanted help from France, because France had fought the British for a long time.

To get France to help, Congress had Franklin go to Paris to talk to the French for the colonists. At the time, Franklin was over 70 years old and was sick. A lot of people were afraid he would not be able to go.

Franklin decided he would go. The French loved Franklin. He had visited France while he was working in London. He had even met King Louis. He was friends with many French politicians.

Benjamin Franklin in a fur hat

Franklin was the best person to talk to the French. Franklin did the right amount of working and playing. He once said, "If you would persuade, you must appeal to interest rather than intellect."

News of an important America victory finally reached France. The colonists won the Battle of Saratoga in 1777. This helped Franklin get the French to join the war with the colonies. France started helping in 1778.

Franklin stayed in France until 1785. He helped get the French to spend money on the colonists and help them win the Revolution. Congress awarded Franklin when the war ended. They chose him as Minister to France. Franklin later signed the Treaty of Paris between the United States and Great Britain. This ended the Revolutionary War and made America free.

Chapter 6: The Constitutional Convention of 1787

A painting of Franklin coming home to Philadelphia

In 1785, Franklin was almost 80 years old. He decided to come home to Philadelphia. He knew that he had little time left, but his public life was not over. He was elected the President of Pennsylvania. This was similar to being a governor. He had trouble doing all the work.

In 1787, the states sent people to Philadelphia to talk about changing the government. Franklin was chosen by Pennsylvania. He didn't do much during the summer. He was mostly quiet and did little in debate. But he was present at meetings. He introduced an anti-slavery clause to the convention.

On the last day of the Convention, September 17, 1787, the Constitution was signed. Franklin gave a speech explaining why he would vote in favor of it:

"I confess that there are several parts of this constitution which I do not at present approve, but I am not sure I shall never approve them: For having lived long, I have experienced many instances of being obliged by better information, or fuller consideration, to change opinions even on important subjects, which I once thought right, but found to be otherwise. It is therefore that the older I grow, the more apt I am to doubt my own judgment, and to pay more respect to the judgment of others… In these sentiments, Sir, I agree to this Constitution with all its faults, if they are such; because I think a general Government necessary for us, and there is no form of Government but what may be a blessing to the people if well administered, and believe farther that this is likely to be well administered for a course of years, and can only end in Despotism, as other forms have done before it, when the people shall become so corrupted as to need despotic Government, being incapable of any other. I doubt too whether any other Convention we can obtain, may be able to make a better Constitution. For when you assemble a number of men to have the advantage of their joint wisdom, you inevitably assemble with those men, all their prejudices, their passions, their errors of opinion, their local interests, and their selfish views. From such an assembly can a perfect production be expected? It therefore astonishes me, Sir, to find this system approaching so near to perfection as it does; and I think it will astonish our enemies, who are waiting with confidence to hear that our councils are confounded like those of the Builders of Babel; and that our States are on the point of separation, only to meet hereafter for the purpose of cutting one another's throats. Thus I consent, Sir, to this Constitution because I expect no better, and because I am not sure, that it is not the best. The opinions I have had of its errors, I sacrifice to the public good. I have never whispered a syllable of them abroad. Within these walls they were born, and here they shall die."

Chapter 7: Franklin's Final Years

Franklin was the only man to sign the Declaration of Independence, the Treaty of Alliance with France, the Treaty of Paris, and the Constitution. He finally got to stop working now. In 1788, he wrote his autobiography. He also became President of the Pennsylvania Abolitionist Society. He fought against slavery and gave speeches on the subject. In 1787, Franklin helped create a college named in his honor: Franklin and Marshall College in Lancaster, Pennsylvania.

Benjamin Franklin had been ill in both the 1770s and 1780s. He was a very old man by 1790. His great life was coming to an end. On April 17th, 1790, Benjamin Franklin died. He was buried in the Christ Church Burial Grounds in Philadelphia. More than 20,000 mourners gathered in Philadelphia to witness his funeral. It was the biggest public gathering the city had ever seen.

Benjamin Franklin was a smart writer, a great scientist, a good diplomat, and one of the most important leaders of the Revolution. He is probably the most famous non-President in American history. He will always be one of the most popular Founding Fathers.

George Washington

Chapter 1: Washington's Early Life and Education, 1732 – 1753

George Washington was born on February 22, 1732. His parents were Augustine and Mary Washington. They lived in Virginia, and George was raised to view himself as a Virginian. The family was still loyal to Britain.

Augustine Washington

George had an older brother named Lawrence. When Augustine died, Lawrence received lots of land and 50 slaves. 11 year old George only received a small farm and ten slaves. Lawrence allowed George to move in with him at his home, Mount Vernon. There, George received a short education. It focused on subjects like mathematics and surveying. The Washingtons thought this suited the young George. He would need to make a living.

Mount Vernon

    Washington earned fame as a general during the American Revolution, but his family thought military life would be too harsh for him. They kept him from joining the British Navy when he was young. Instead, surveying the land of Virginia was a fitting career for Washington. Virginia was still largely wild and unknown. In 1748, 16 year old Washington started to be a surveyor. Measuring Virginia's land proved to be the stepping stone for him.

    Washington learned about the best land in Virginia. In 1750, he bought land in the Ohio Valley. Over the next few years, he bought more land. By the time he died, he owned even more than his brother Lawrence!

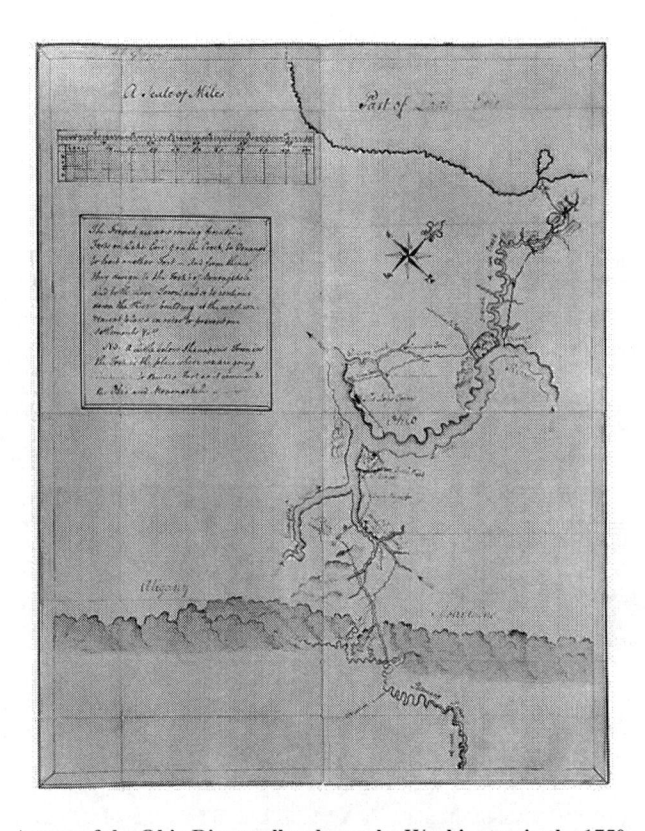

A map of the Ohio River valley drawn by Washington in the 1750s

Success did not come quickly. Washington's career stopped in 1751 when his brother got sick. The two brothers traveled to Barbados. They hoped the warm climate would help him, but Lawrence did not get better. George also got sick with smallpox. Many people died from it, but George got better.

When George was better, he and Lawrence returned to Mount Vernon. Lawrence died in 1752. He left his home to his wife and daughter. George was next in line. Lawrence's daughter died in 1754, and his wife died in 1761. Then George gained Mount Vernon.

Washington was now on his way to success. He had land and wealth. But that was not enough. He needed a good career, so he joined the army.

Chapter 2: The French & Indian War

George Washington as a British soldier

Washington is the Father of Our Country, but first he was a British soldier. George fought for the British in the Seven Years' War. The war was fought by France and Great Britain. The fighting in North America was called The French & Indian War.

Washington was famous for his calmness. He was also a very hard worker. Virginia's Governor made George a major in the Virginia militia. In 1753, the British and French had a border dispute. It took place along the Ohio River near Pennsylvania. The French were building forts on land the British claimed. The British decided to demand that they stop.

That October, the Governor sent a 22 year old George to deliver the demand. He carried the letter from the governor to the French. Washington knew about the French forces. He decided to do more than just deliver a letter.

Washington used his trip to help the British and himself. He spoke carefully to the Indians. He wanted them to support the British cause. He also talked to the French to see what was going on.

He told people about the French military posts between New Orleans and the Great Lakes. He also explored the Forks of the Ohio. He found a good site for building a fort. He even reported on the new French forts. He guessed their strength and how ready they were for war.

All of this information helped George and the British. Washington demanded that the French leave Ohio. The French were not interested in moving. Washington delivered the message in December of 1753. War broke out in early 1754. Washington wrote about his trip, and people read it in America and England. Washington was now known by all his countrymen.

The French didn't back down. Washington led a small group back to the region to fight the French. Washington's small group came upon a group of French troops in Pennsylvania and attacked them. The French complained that he unfairly attacked by surprise. In July 1754, a French unit attacked Washington's men and captured Washington. He signed something in French, which he did not understand. It said that England was wrong. It also said they would not return for a year.

This started the French & Indian War. Both countries fought hard. They sent thousands of troops into America over the next two years. Washington wrote a description of his first battle with the French. Readers loved it. He was made a Colonel. He was also sent to the front lines of the fighting.

There were many defeats for the British. In 1755, Major General Edward Braddock set out for the Ohio River Valley. He hoped to take the region from the French. Instead, the trip was a disaster. They lost the Battle of Monongahela, and Braddock was killed there. But Washington survived and became a hero. He rallied the troops as they ran away in disorder.

In 1758, the war turned for the British. The Royal Army captured Fort Duquesne from the French. Washington led the Virginia soldiers until the British won the war. After the war, Britain had almost all of North America.

Washington learned about fighting on American land. He also became familiar with British military tactics. He even learned about how to train soldiers. This would help in another war later.

Washington wanted to keep being a soldier, but he would not be paid. Washington decided to do something else again. In 1758, George married Martha Custis. Martha was a widow with two children. She was also very rich.

Portrait of Martha in 1757

Washington turned to politics and was elected to the Virginia state legislature. He divided his time between politics and planting. Mount Vernon was a growing tobacco plantation. This increased his fortune. By 1760, he was one of Virginia's richest and most powerful men.

Chapter 3: Trouble with Britain

The French and Indian War was a success for Great Britain. Still, the war put the kingdom deep in debt. Parliament began to pass new taxes to repay the nation's war debts. Many of the new taxes targeted the 13 colonies. The war had begun in North America. Many of Britain's war expenses had been to defend the colonies.

Many believed that Parliament had no right to raise taxes. Parliament had no American members. The colonists argued that they could not raise taxes on them. The new tax acts began in 1765 with the Stamp Act. The Stamp Act said that paper used for printing must carry a valid stamp. This would show that a tax had been paid to the British.

The Stamp Act was the first tax that Parliament passed. It was repealed in 1766. Then Parliament passed an act giving itself the power to tax the colonies. This angered the colonists who just fought the Stamp Act.

The tax acts continued in 1767. The Revenue Act of 1767 taxed items that came to the colonies. Americans did not like the Revenue Act either.

Parliament passed the Quartering Act of 1765. It forced people in the colonies to let British soldiers live in their houses. The soldiers could stay for free in inns, barns or public houses. Parliament assumed that the colonies would build places for the troops. That did not happen.

Washington did not like Britain's taxes. His close friend, George Mason, helped him understand what the British were doing. Washington spent his time in the Virginia legislature listening to others.

George Mason

Washington did not like the 1765 Stamp Act. He also disagreed with the Coercive Acts of 1774. These followed the Boston Tea Party. The British Parliament passed a series of acts to punish Boston, and the colony of Massachusetts. They closed Boston's harbor. Parliament hoped to force the colonies to obey them. Instead, colonists were even more angry. Many colonists viewed the acts as a violation of their rights. In 1774, they organized the First Continental Congress. It met in Philadelphia to coordinate a protest.

Washington was selected to join the Congress. Washington and 55 other men fought against the Intolerable Acts. They declared that they had rights. They also talked about a boycott on the British. The First Continental Congress asked the British government to end the Intolerable Acts. They also agreed to meet again next summer.

Chapter 4: The American Revolution

Massachusetts was a problem for Britain. It began with the Boston Massacre in 1770. Then came the Boston Tea Party in December 1773. After this, the British put a military command in place over Boston.

In early 1775, General Thomas Gage heard that colonists had weapons in Concord, Massachusetts. Gage sent 700 British soldiers to take the weapons. Patriot leaders heard about this. Men warned the people of Lexington and Concord the night before.

General Gage

The local militia met the British soldiers at Lexington. Shots were fired and some colonists were killed. The British soldiers marched to Concord. There they met more armed colonists. Colonists came from other places to fight the British as they marched back to Boston. Many British soldiers died trying to get back to Boston. The American Revolution had begun.

The pleas of the First Continental Congress had no effect on King George III or Parliament. The Second Continental Congress decided to convene in June, 1775. By then, colonists had taken things into their own hands. The First Continental Congress had met for 6 months. The Second Continental Congress would last for 6 years.

Washington had gone to the First Continental Congress. He was also chosen for the Second Continental Congress in 1775. Washington always wore his military uniform to meetings. This let people know he was ready for command. He was still famous for his military career in the 1750s.

On June 14th, 1775, the Congress chose 43 year old Washington to lead the Continental Army. He accepted the position on June 16th at the age of 43. The following day, the bloodiest battle of the whole Revolution would be fought. It happened at Bunker Hill, across the Charles River from Boston. The Battle of Bunker Hill helped make the colonial soldiers feel better about themselves. They continued to surround Boston and trap the British there.

Washington joined the Continental Army around Boston after the Battle of Bunker Hill. The first things he learned about were problems his army faced. The army had little military supplies or gunpowder. They were not very able to make much more. This was a problem during the entire war. Washington spent the first year of the war organizing his army.

Washington once lined up logs around Boston to look like cannons. Later he replaced them with real guns. This caused the British to leave the city in March 1776.

Washington knew the British were going to move by sea to New York City. He marched his army south to defend the city. New York City did not have good ground for Washington to fight from. Washington wasn't sure about defending the city. Congress demanded that he stay and fight.

Washington did what he was told. In the summer of 1776, the British landed 20,000 troops near New York City. British General William Howe captured Staten Island. Washington tried to fight, but his army was nearly captured. He retreated across New York City. Many of his troops were so scared that they left the army. Others were sick. Washington was ashamed. He also felt betrayed by both his troops and Congress.

Washington escaped New York City in the middle of the night. This saved his army. The British chased Washington and his army west across New Jersey into Pennsylvania. Congress fled from Philadelphia. Washington's Continental Army lost over 5,000 men during its retreat. He now had fewer than 5,000 soldiers. He didn't have enough men to fight the British. Now they were feeling bad too. Washington had to worry about his army leaving at the end of the year.

The British camped out in New Jersey during the winter. Washington knew he needed a big victory. On Christmas night, Washington led his troops across the freezing Delaware River. They marched to Trenton. There they attacked the soldiers stationed there.

Washington crossing the Delaware River

Painting of the Battle of Trenton

The British general, Lord Cornwallis, marched south with an army to take back Trenton. Washington marched his army to get behind Cornwallis. He attacked the British at Princeton, New Jersey and won. This forced the British to retreat to New York City.

Trumbull's painting of Washington at Trenton

In 1777, Washington tried to surround the British army as it marched on Philadelphia. He failed. At the Battle of Germantown, he was defeated, On October 19th, 1777, the British entered Philadelphia. The Continental Congress fled again.

Washington's men settled in winter quarters at Valley Forge, Pennsylvania. His army was not very organized. Congress even considered replacing Washington as Commander in Chief. Washington was very upset, and the winter was very cold. 2,000 men died in camp from diseases.

Washington's headquarters at Valley Forge

Still, Washington helped train and build a better army at Valley Forge. He started a better training program for his troops. The Continental Army left Valley Forge better than ever.

Depiction of Washington and the Marquis de Lafayette at Valley Forge

The British built up Yorktown on the York River in Virginia. Washington decided in 1781 to move south toward Virginia. Washington pretended to move toward New York. Then he turned his army south to Virginia.

When Washington arrived in Yorktown, it was surrounded. Over 7,000 British officers and soldiers were captured. It was the last major battle in North America. Cornwallis surrendered to Washington, handing him his sword.

Cornwallis' surrender did not officially end the war in 1781. During 1782 and 1783, Washington moved his army back up to New York City. He made sure his army was on guard and ready to fight.

The war finally ended in 1783. Washington resigned as a soldier. On December 23, 1783, he broke up his armies. This protected the new nation.

Chapter 5: The Constitutional Convention of 1787

Washington wanted to retire. He moved back to Mount Vernon and enjoyed building his farm. This did not last long. The new United States had a lot of trouble after the war because it was very weak. Congress did not have the power to tax. They could only ask for money from the states. The United States had no navy and American ships were attacked by pirates. Congress could do nothing to stop the attacks. It could not raise money for a navy.

Congress was unable to pay its debts. If they did not pay these debts, other countries would not trust them. Congress had to find a way to raise money. This meant changing the government. Each state sent men to Philadelphia to discuss this problem. One of these men was George Washington. He was made the head of the meeting, which was called the Constitutional Convention.

The men worked together to create a new government. It would have the right to tax. It would also have a president. It created our Constitution on September 17, 1787.

Chapter 6: President Washington

The Constitution said that the country should have a president. Everyone agreed that Washington should be the new president. He won every vote. He became president on April 30, 1789 in New York City.

After he became president, he made a speech. He said American needed to unite as one country. He said "the foundation of our national policy will be laid in the pure and immutable principles of private morality, and the preeminence of free government be exemplified by all the attributes which can win the affection of its citizens and command the respect of the world."

One of the first things Washington did was to create a Cabinet. He chose a group of men he trusted to advise him. He asked them to advise him on money, politics, defense and law.

Washington worked hard. He arranged for laws to pass that would pay his soldiers. He also insisted that the government start paying off its debts.

Washington's advisers often disagreed with each other. Alexander Hamilton and Thomas Jefferson were working for Washington, but they disagreed on politics. Soon they started dividing into two different sides. These two sides would become the first two political parties in America.

Thomas Jefferson

Alexander Hamilton

Washington did not like political parties. He thought men should do what was right without thinking about other's opinions. As president, he sometimes sided with one side. Another time he sided with the other side. Many times he made his own path.

Washington also tried to work with both sides and bring them together. He talked to both sides about working together. He said that each side should give a little. That way they could find an answer that everyone could agree on.

One of the things that Washington helped work out was where the new capital city would be. Finally, they chose a place near Mount Vernon. It was on the banks of the Potomac River. At first, it was called the District of Columbia. Later it would be named after President Washington himself.

The next issue that concerned Washington was what to do about money. America was a growing country. It needed a way to provide businesses with money. It also had to have a way to manage how much money it printed.

Alexander Hamilton was concerned about this. He was the Secretary of Treasury, and he wanted the United States to have a national bank. He said this would be a good way to control the money. Other people disagreed. Thomas Jefferson was the Secretary of State. Jefferson said that a national bank would have too much power.

The Constitution did not have an answer for the debate, but it did give Congress the right to control buying and selling. Since that requires money, it was decided that Congress could create a bank. Washington tried to keep everyone happy. He was not sure who he agreed with. What he did know was that arguing made the country weaker.

Washington never said what he believed about the bank. Instead, he said that money was a decision for the Secretary of Treasury. That was Alexander Hamilton. Since Hamilton wanted a bank, Washington would too. Jefferson was angry about Washington's decision. He felt that his old friend had let him down. The two friends grew apart.

While Washington was president, the Bill of Rights was passed. It became part of the Constitution. In 1792, Washington was elected president again.

After Washington was elected, France declared war on Great Britain and much of Europe. America was divided between Great Britain and France. France had been a strong friend for colonists in the American Revolution, but many Americans preferred the British. Jefferson liked France. Hamilton liked Great Britain.

On April 22nd, 1793, Washington put out the Neutrality Proclamation. It said that America would not take sides. It would be at peace with both France and Britain. This was a lasting mark of Washington. Jefferson was angry. He felt Washington sided with Hamilton too much. Jefferson never spoke to Washington again.

In 1791, Congress passed a tax on liquor. Washington signed the bill into law. At first, it did not seem important. By the summer of 1794, it was a problem. From July until November, small farmers from Pennsylvania fought the tax. They said the tax was like Britain's Stamp Act of 1765. They even killed a federal officer.

Washington was worried. He could not allow violence against the government. It hurt the new American government. Washington called on the military to stop the rebellion. He even led the force himself. This made him the only president in history to lead a military force. The rebellion was put down. Americans were confident in the government again.

Another crisis soon began. The President sent Chief Justice of the Supreme Court, John Jay, to Britain. He told Jay to stop the British Navy from taking American ships. Jay returned in 1795 with a treaty. Some people did not like it. Britain offered to leave its forts on the borders of America. They also agreed to pay for damage done to American ships. Britain demanded that the young America repay its debts to Britain. They also agreed to let Americans trade in the West Indies if America would let Britain trade for fur.

John Jay

Jefferson did not like the treaty. He thought not trading with Great Britain would be a good idea. He also felt that Britain should pay Southern planters for slaves lost on the ships taken by the British. But the treaty passed, and Washington liked it.

Others argued that the Constitution only let the House of Representatives raise taxes. Since the treaty made America pay Britain, the House claimed it had to vote on it. Washington disagreed. He said the Constitution gave the power to negotiate treaties only to the President and the Senate. Washington won the debate.

By 1796, Washington was tired of being President. He wanted to return to Mount Vernon. He was sad about the fighting in the government. But he had one more job to do. On September 17th, 1796, Washington gave his "Farewell Address." In this speech, he gave the country his wise advice.

Washington made three points in his speech. First, he warned the United States against getting mixed up in other country's problems. Second, he warned the country against fighting among themselves. Third, he praised personal morality. He said honesty was important for good government. America followed the first point and the third point, but not the second point. The second point led to the Civil War almost 100 years later.

Chapter 7: The Father of Our Country

Washington left Philadelphia in March of 1797. He returned to Mount Vernon to retire. This did not last. The new President, John Adams, feared that war with Britain was going to start again. He asked Washington to serve as the head of the armies. Washington agreed. He served from July of 1798 until his death. The two dies would not end up fighting though.

On December 12, 1799, Washington worked for hours in snow and sleet. His clothes were soaked. He wore them through the evening as he ate dinner. He got a sore throat. The next morning he was much worse. To help him, the doctors drew a lot of his blood out of his body. They thought this would help him get better. Instead, it made him worse. On December 14th, 1799, Washington died. He was 67 years old.

Washington was buried in a tomb at his home in Mount Vernon. Today, millions of people visit the house and the tomb. Most are from America but many come from other parts of the world. They want to pay their respects to America's first president.

One man described Washington best when he said, "First in war, first in peace, and first in the hearts of his countrymen."

George's and Martha's Tombs at Mount Vernon

True or False?

George Washington is the Father of Our Country, and one of the greatest presidents. A lot of Americans who admired him made up stories about Washington that others liked. The stories kept spreading around until almost everybody thought they were true.

Did George Washington Have False Teeth? A lot of people think Washington never smiled for portraits because he had wooden teeth. Washington did not have wooden teeth. But he did have false teeth. The teeth were made of ivory and metal. It caused a lot of mouth pain.

Did George Washington Chop Down His Father's Cherry Tree? One legend says that George Washington could never tell a lie. Washington proved it by telling his dad the truth when his dad asked if George chopped down a cherry tree. This story was made up by Parson Mason Weems, who wrote about Washington in the early 1800s.

Did George Washington Throw a Silver Dollar across the Potomac? One story said Washington was so strong that he could throw a silver dollar across the Potomac River. Washington was a very strong man, but nobody can do that. The Potomac River is over a mile wide. Also, silver dollars didn't exist yet while Washington was alive.

The Washington Monument

Thomas Jefferson

Chapter 1: Early Life

Thomas Jefferson was born in Shadwell, Virginia. Both his parents were involved in politics. His mother was from the Randolph family. They held offices in the Virginian government. His father founded the town Thomas was born in.

Jefferson was trained for greatness from the very beginning. His education was one of the best in the world. Jefferson started school at the age of 5. He studied with private teachers. They taught him Latin and Greek. He also studied philosophy, science, violin and dance.

In 1760, at age 17, Jefferson attended the College of William and Mary. He studied law and became a lawyer in Virginia in 1767.

Jefferson's father died in 1757. His estate was split between Thomas and his brother. Thomas received about 5,000 acres of land and 20-40 slaves. He was only 14 at the time. He was not able to control his own property for seven years.

When he was 21, Jefferson began building his own house. He had some knowledge of architecture, so he designed his home himself. He named it Monticello. He began working on it in 1768, but he did not finish it for a long time.

Jefferson moved into Monticello in 1770. His wife, Martha, joined him there in 1772. Martha was from a wealthy Virginian background. They went on to have six children. Sadly, only one lived to be older than 25.

Monticello

Jefferson worked as a lawyer during the 1760's and 70's. Jefferson's family was very rich, so Jefferson did not need to work for an income. This gave him time to think and read.

In 1769, Jefferson began to enter politics. First, he won a seat in the Virginia state legislature. Jefferson joined the House of Burgesses, which was the first body comprised of elected representatives in the 13 colonies. It was a place for fierce debate.

The British Parliament had placed several types of taxes on the American colonies. One of the ways they did this was with the Stamp Act of 1765. It required that many printed materials be printed on stamped paper. This paper was produced in London. Jefferson heard Patrick Henry argue against the Stamp Act. Later, he had his turn when Parliament passed the Coercive Acts in 1774. These were issued in response to the Boston Tea Party of December 1773.

Patrick Henry

The Coercive Acts angered the colonies. Jefferson wrote a series of papers protesting them. He later wrote *A Summary View on the Rights of British Americans*. Jefferson wrote about self-government, law, and rights.

Chapter 2: The American Revolution

In 1775, men from 12 colonies met in Philadelphia. The 56 men met to write a response to the Coercive Acts. They considered forming a boycott of British trade. They also declared their rights. Jefferson was not one of the men, but he did offer advice. His book gave the Congress something to think about. The First Continental Congress asked the British to end the Intolerable Acts. They then agreed to meet again the following summer.

Massachusetts was a problem for Britain. It began with the Boston Massacre in 1770. Then came the Boston Tea Party in December 1773. After this, the British put a military command in place over Boston.

In early 1775, General Thomas Gage heard that colonists had weapons in Concord, Massachusetts. Gage sent 700 British soldiers to take the weapons. Patriot leaders heard about this. Men warned the people of Lexington and Concord the night before.

General Gage

   The local militia met the British soldiers at Lexington. Shots were fired and some colonists were killed. The British soldiers marched to Concord. There they met more armed colonists. Colonists came from other places to fight the British as they marched back to Boston. Many British soldiers died trying to get back to Boston. The American Revolution had begun.

   The pleas of the First Continental Congress had no effect on King George III or Parliament. The Second Continental Congress decided to convene in June, 1775. By then, colonists had taken things into their own hands. The First Continental Congress had met for 6 months. The Second Continental Congress would last for 6 years.

   On June 17, 1775, the bloodiest battle of the whole Revolution was fought. It happened at Bunker Hill, across the Charles River from Boston. The Battle of Bunker Hill helped make the colonial soldiers feel better about themselves. They continued to surround Boston and trap the British there.

   Some delegates tried to think of ways the colonies could get along with the Britain. Soon they began to think independence was best.

In 1775, Jefferson published *Notes on the State of Virginia.* In it he talked more about what he had discussed in his first book. He also talked about living on a farm. He said it was better than living in a city.

The most important thing Jefferson did was write the Declaration of Independence. At age 33, Jefferson was the youngest delegate at the Second Continental Congress. Because of this, he rarely spoke. In fact, he was a poor public speaker.

Trumbull's famous painting of Jefferson presenting a draft of the Declaration of Independence to Congress

Jefferson shined with his writing. The Congress chose five men to write a document explaining why they wanted independence. Everyone agreed that Jefferson should write it.

Writing the Declaration was the most important moment in Jefferson's life. He wrote

> "We hold these truths to be self-evident, that all men are created equal, that they are endowed by their Creator with certain unalienable Rights, that among these are Life, Liberty and the pursuit of Happiness."

During June of 1776, Jefferson worked in Philadelphia. He wrote the first rough draft of the Declaration of Independence. It had one strange part. He blamed slavery on King George III and the British. He said:

> "He has waged cruel war against human nature itself, violating its most sacred rights of life and liberty in the persons of a distant people who never offended him, captivating & carrying them into slavery in another hemisphere or to incur miserable death in their transportation thither. This piratical warfare, the opprobrium of infidel powers, is the warfare of the Christian King of Great Britain. Determined to keep open a market where Men should be bought & sold, he has prostituted his negative for suppressing every legislative attempt to prohibit or restrain this execrable commerce."

Most of the people in Congress disagreed with this and made Jefferson change it. Then they voted on the entire document. They passed it on July 4, 1776. July 4 became Independence Day.

Jefferson was also concerned about Virginia. In September, he went home to serve in his home state. He spent time writing a constitution for the State of Virginia. The constitution gave every adult male in Virginia 50 acres of land. He also worked on a law banning the slave trade in Virginia. This made Virginia the first state to ban the slave trade.

A year later, Jefferson was elected Governor of Virginia. He was 36 years old. His election came at a difficult time. The country was at war with Britain. Much of Jefferson's two terms were focused on fighting British forces around the state.

Jefferson was not a good governor. He was too impatient. Also, he did not have much power. Jefferson learned not to like the limits he put on his own power.

Chapter 3: Serving His Country

In October 1781, the British surrendered to General George Washington at Yorktown. Over the next two years, the British and Americans made peace. Jefferson rejoined the Continental Congress beginning in 1783. He served one important year. Although he owned slaves, he wanted there to be no slavery in America.

George Washington

In 1784, Jefferson became America's new ambassador to France. It was a good job for him. He spoke French well and liked the people. Still, it was a challenge for him. Many countries thought that the United States would fail. Others thought it could not continue to operate financially. They said it would fall without the support of Great Britain. The French were upset that America was not paying them back the money they had loaned her during the Revolution.

Jefferson had to work with diplomats in other countries. They needed to build a good image of the United States. He got along well with John Adams, who was serving in Great Britain. During the 1780s, the two developed a friendship. They wrote letters to each other for years.

John Adams

   Jefferson did not serve only in France. His main role was to get other countries to trade with America. In Prussia, he made a treaty with Frederick the Great. He also visited London. There he helped Adams try to make a similar treaty with King George III. This did not work out.

   Because Jefferson was in Europe, he was not at the Constitutional Convention in 1787. Still, he did follow the debates and wrote letters. He wrote a lot to his friend James Madison, reminding him to work on protecting people's rights. Madison is known as the "Father of the Constitution".

James Madison

Jefferson enjoyed his time in Europe. He loved seeing the art and the buildings. He studied them closely. This gave him ideas on how to expand Monticello. He also watched the French Revolution unfold around him. Jefferson left France in 1789. He returned to the United States to serve as Secretary of State.

Chapter 4: President George Washington

The Constitution said that the country should have a president. Everyone agreed that Washington should be the new president. He won every vote. He became president on April 30, 1789 in New York City.

After he became president, he made a speech. He said American needed to unite as one country. He said "the foundation of our national policy will be laid in the pure and immutable principles of private morality, and the preeminence of free government be exemplified by all the attributes which can win the affection of its citizens and command the respect of the world."

One of the first things Washington did was to create a Cabinet. He chose a group of men he trusted to advise him. He asked them to advise him on money, politics, defense and law. George Washington asked Thomas Jefferson to serve as the Secretary of State. Jefferson's time in office was unusual. Most Secretaries of State worked on issues with other countries, but Jefferson was busy with other things.

Jefferson's ideas were not always the same as President Washington's. America was policy focused on France and Britain. Britain and France were often at war with one another, and President Washington wanted to stay out of their fighting. He told Jefferson to support this policy, but Jefferson wanted to be closer friends with France. He said that was right because they had helped America fight the British. Jefferson didn't like the British.

Another man in Washington's cabinet had different ideas. He was the Secretary of the Treasury, Alexander Hamilton. Hamilton and Jefferson often fought for Washington's favor. Jefferson often felt left out. He became angry. He resigned from Washington's cabinet in 1793.

Alexander Hamilton

Other men in the government did not like Hamilton. There men included Madison, Aaron Burr and DeWitt Clinton. In 1791, Jefferson began meeting with them. They agreed to team up against Hamilton. Jefferson thought that states should have the most power. Hamilton thought the federal government should be more powerful.

Another problem was in how each man saw the economy. Hamilton believed in business. Jefferson liked farming. Hamilton wanted to see America full of busy cities. Jefferson wanted the countryside to be covered in peaceful farms.

Hamilton convinced Washington to create a national bank. It would loan money to new businesses. It would also helped the United States pay off its war debts. Jefferson did not like the national bank. He was afraid of the federal government having too much power.

The arguments between Jefferson and Hamilton led to something new. They created the two party political system. During the 1790's, Jefferson and Madison began making the Democratic-

Republican Party. Hamilton and John Adams made the Federalist Party. Jefferson's people were mostly from the South. The Federalists were in the North.

Jefferson thought he'd retire to his plantation. He planned to keep working on Monticello. He wanted nothing more to do with politics. He wanted to spend his time reading and thinking. He was happiest on his plantation and did not like life in the big city.

However, the party he created wanted him to run for President in 1796. He won the nomination. Still, he was not too excited about the idea. He came in second against his old friend John Adams. Coming in second place made Jefferson the Vice President.

In the 1790s, being Vice President didn't include many duties. The first Vice President, John Adams, once said, "My country has in its wisdom contrived for me the most insignificant office that ever the invention of man contrived or his imagination conceived."

The main duty of the Vice-President was to act as President of the Senate. Jefferson wrote a manual about how to properly operate in the Congress. It is still used today.

In 1798, Congress passed four laws known as the Alien and Sedition Acts. These laws made Jefferson and his friends very angry.

The first was The Naturalization Act. It required people in the United States to wait 14 years before becoming citizens. Next was The Alien Enemies Act. It let the President make foreigners he did not like leave. Then came the Sedition Act. It said that people were not allowed to talk badly about the country's leaders.

These laws were targeted at Jefferson's Democratic-Republican party. The Federalists thought they were too critical of their work. The only people convicted were those who were against fighting the French. Jefferson and his friends liked the French. 10 newspaper editors were convicted. They had to pay a lot of money in fines. A Congressman from Vermont was jailed for writing something against President Adams.

Jefferson and Madison worked against the acts. They tried to say that states that disagreed with a federal law did not have to follow it. This opened the door for states to not enforce any laws they did not like.

Chapter 5: President Jefferson

Although Jefferson and Adams often argued, they were still friends. Sadly, this ended with the Election of 1800. Jefferson won the election, beating Adams. Adams went back to Boston without saying goodbye to Jefferson. He only left him a note about the White House stables behind. The two men did not speak to each other for another 12 years.

Jefferson's election to the Presidency was unusual. The Democratic-Republicans had two nominees, Jefferson and Burr. The plan was that Burr would be Jefferson's Vice President. That meant that Jefferson would win, and Burr would come in second.

Then there was a mix-up. Someone voted the wrong way and the two men tied. The House of Representatives had to break the tie. Many voted for Burr. The first 35 ballots were always a tie between Burr and Jefferson. Finally, Jefferson's old political enemy, Alexander Hamilton, spoke in favor of Jefferson. This helped Jefferson win. Burr was so angry that he later killed Hamilton in a duel.

Aaron Burr

Thomas Jefferson was sworn in as the third President of the United States on March 4th, 1801. He was the first president to take the oath of office in Washington, D.C. This was only right, since he had fought hard to have the nation's capital move there.

Right after Jefferson became president, a tiny little nation declared war on the United States. On May 14th, 1801, the Pasha of Tripoli declared war on America. He was angry because Jefferson refused to give him more than $80,000. The two sides had a treaty that promised America would pay $80,000.

The United States had already paid nearly $2 million dollars to North African nations. This was so they would allow American ships to do business in their territory. America never declared war on Tripoli, but Jefferson sent navy ships to the area. The First Barbary War officially ended in 1805.

At the end of the year, Jefferson had to inform Congress of the State of the Union. Washington and Adams always made speeches before the Congress. Jefferson simply sent a note. Every President followed this pattern until Woodrow Wilson in 1913. He went back to making a speech. Now all presidents make speeches.

The best thing that Jefferson did was make the Louisiana Purchase. This was not easy. The area was part of a conflict between France and Spain. Spain owned land on the west coast of North America. This area surrounded the Mississippi River. France gave the land to Spain after the French and Indian War. In 1800, France's emperor, Napoleon, got the land back. Spain traded it to him for another piece of land.

Napoleon did not keep up his side of the deal, and the Spanish became angry. They stopped all trade with the French on the Mississippi River. This hurt the United States. The country did not own the river, but they needed it to trade.

Before he became president, Jefferson had done two things that helped him. First, he wrote the Declaration of Independence. Also, he was an American diplomat in France. He put the skills he learned to good use. They helped him make the Louisiana Purchase.

Jefferson sent his friend James Monroe to France. Monroe met Napoleon at just the right time. Napoleon's armies were failing in the West Indies. He was hoping to focus more on Europe. That is why he was open to selling the Louisiana Territory.

The United States paid 15 million dollars to France. The Louisiana Purchase gave us all or part of 15 current states. The purchase doubled the size of the United States. Today the land Jefferson bought makes up about one-fourth, or 25%, of all the United States. It also added 92,345 people to the country.

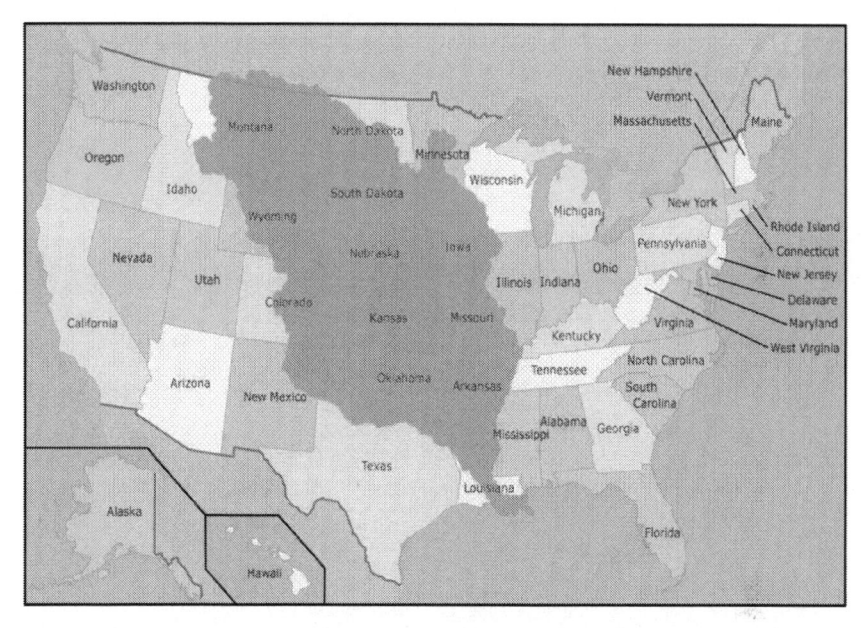

The land bought in the Louisiana Purchase is in green

The purchase was the best moment of Jefferson's life as president. Still, his enemies did not like it. They did not think the Constitution gave the President the authority to buy land. But this did not stop Jefferson. Although he felt that the Constitution did not contain any provisions for acquiring territory, Jefferson thought it was too important.

Napoleon was happy to sell America the land. He said, "This accession of territory affirms forever the power of the United States, and I have given England a maritime rival who sooner or later will humble her pride."

In August 1803, Jefferson sent two men to explore the new territory he had bought. They would explore both the Louisiana Territory and the land beyond it. They would also look for waterways. These would allow the United States to trade with Asia. Jefferson also wanted to learn more about the area's natural resources.

Jefferson chose Meriwether Lewis and William Clark to lead the expedition. He saw this as part of a long term goal. He wanted to see the United States expand west across North America. He knew that other countries had not yet claimed the Northwest Territory. He hoped to claim that Americans had "discovered" the land. This would make them the owners of it.

From 1804-1806, Lewis and Clark traveled west. They depended on local Indian tribes for help. They formed friendships with over two dozen Indian nations. They were able to return home to Missouri rather quickly using the rivers they had discovered. The rivers made traveling easier and faster.

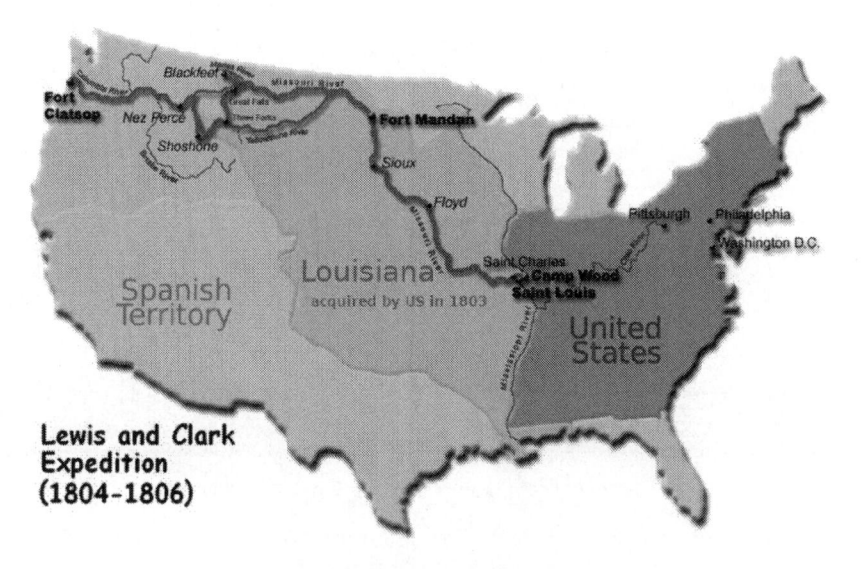

The route Lewis and Clark traveled in red

The Louisiana Purchase made Jefferson very popular. He was ready to run for re-election. Still, Congress needed to prevent a problem similar to what happened in 1800. Another tie would be bad. Congress passed the 12th Amendment on December 12, 1803. It made separate ballots for President and Vice-President. Jefferson won the election of 1804 easily.

Jefferson's second term in office was not as important as his first. Still, he did have to deal with some problems. The British Navy was good at controlling ships on the oceans around the world. They often stopped American ships. They would then capture sailors and force them to serve in the British Navy. In April of 1806, Congress was so angry that it stopped the British from trading some goods in America.

Matters got worse when Napoleon got involved in November of 1806. French ships were also being searched by the British Navy, so France stopped all trade with Great Britain. They said they would block all ships trading with the British. This included the American ships that still traded with Britain. Jefferson now had to deal with two nations stopping American trade in

Europe.

In 1807, the British Navy stopped an American ship called the *Chesapeake*. The ship's crew refused to allow the British to search their ship. The British opened fire and sunk the ship. This made Jefferson and the American public very angry. Jefferson told Congress to pass a total embargo of all trade with European nations. They did in December of 1807.

The Embargo Act was a huge failure for Jefferson. It was also a disaster for the United States. It solved the problem of kidnapped sailors, but it cost America a lot of money. For France and Great Britain, American trade not important. But for America, trade with those two nations was a huge part of the economy.

The Embargo did lead to one good thing. It allowed Jefferson to ban the slave trade. He convinced Congress to outlaw importing new slaves from Africa. In 1808, Congress passed a ban on the African slave trade. This meant that bringing slaves into America was banned. But it did not prevent the owning or trading of slaves already in the country.

By 1809, the Embargo Act had become too much. Jefferson realized the pain the Act had caused the nation. Congress repealed the Act in March. It made a new law that allowed trade with all nations except Britain and France. Three years later, Britain and America were fighting the War of 1812 against each other.

Chapter 6: Final Years

Jefferson chose not to run for reelection in 1808. He wanted to follow the tradition set by George Washington. His friend James Madison was elected President. This allowed Jefferson's people to keep control of the White House.

Jefferson left office unhappy with politics. He set out to fulfill a new goal. He would create the University of Virginia. Jefferson wanted Americans to be able to go to school. He wanted the University of Virginia to let in both rich and poor students. He paid close attention to the details of the University. He even laid out the grounds of the campus himself.

Jefferson loved to spend money. He never learned to operate on a budget. During the last years of his life, debt was a problem for him. He spent too much money on Monticello and the University were huge. Those used up most of his wealth.

After the election of 1800, Adams and Jefferson stopped speaking to each. More than ten years later, a friend helped the two reconcile. This led to a renewal in their exchange of letters. These are some of the most famous letters in history.

On July 4, 1826, exactly 50 years after the signing of the Declaration of Independence, 90 year old John Adams lay dying. Realizing what day it was, he said "It is a great day." Then he added, "Thomas Jefferson survives."

Adams was wrong. Jefferson had died hours earlier on the very same day. Dying on the 50th anniversary of the Declaration of Independence could not be more fitting for Thomas Jefferson. He considered the Declaration to be one of his most important achievements. On his grave stone, he demanded that it read, *"Here was buried Thomas Jefferson, Author of the Declaration of American Independence, of the Statute of Virginia for Religious Freedom and the Father of the University of Virginia."*

Jefferson's grave

Jefferson's face on Mount Rushmore

James Madison

Chapter 1: Early Years

On March 16, 1751, James Madison was born in his grandparents' home in Port Conway, Virginia. He was the oldest of 12 children. He was named after his father, James Sr.

As a young boy, James was sick a lot. He would also be sick a lot as an adult. This made him scared about his health all the time. But young "Jemmy," as his family called him, had a great childhood. James Sr. was a rich planter. James's mother Nelly was the daughter of a rich planter too. The Madisons owned a lot of land in Virginia. Their best property was their home, called Montpelier. James Sr. had owned it since his father died. When he died, it would go to Jemmy.

Montpelier

Jemmy grew up with many slaves helping on the land and in the house. When his father died, he became the owner of about 100 slaves. Even though he owned slaves, he would later think slavery was very bad. He would also try to make it illegal to bring slaves to America from other countries.

Jemmy's family wanted him to be very smart. As a child, he was taught by private teachers. They taught him languages like Latin. This would help him work on the United States

Constitution. When he was old enough, James attended the College of New Jersey. This school is now known as Princeton University. Alexander Hamilton also went to school there for a little bit of time. Madison learned to read in Hebrew and Greek. He also wrote a few books, like *A Brief System of Logick*. He was one of the smartest people in school.

James worked so hard at school that he did not make many friends. He would also make himself sick by working too hard. He would be so tired that he had no energy. He liked talking to other people about the government though. In the 1760s and 1770s, the American colonies were not happy with Great Britain. Madison kept up with what was going on.

Madison could also be funny. He once wrote to a friend that he had seen "no place so overstocked with Old-Maids as Princeton." Madison studied so hard that he finished college in just two years. He was done at Princeton by 1771 and went back to Virginia in 1772. Even though he had finished school, Madison never stopped studying. He studied the law when he went home. He wanted to go into politics.

Chapter 2: The American Revolution

By 1774, many people in Virginia were talking about the British. They were tired of being told what to do by a country that was so far away. They wanted to form their own government and be in charge of themselves. One Virginian named Patrick Henry became famous for saying, "Give me liberty or give me death!"

Patrick Henry

Madison was very young when he became a politician. His first political office came in 1774, when he was only 23 years old. He became a member of the Orange County Committee of Safety. The Committee of Safety created militias. A militia was a group of men who learned how to fire guns and act like an army. They were very important for the colonies because they would be most of the soldiers who fought the British. By the end of 1774, Madison was busy making a local militia to protect his county.

In 1776, the Continental Congress wrote the Declaration of Independence. The Declaration of Independence said that the colonies would all be free from Great Britain. That year, Madison was elected to the Virginia Convention. This meant he and others would write the state's constitution. Together with George Mason, Madison wrote Virginia's constitution. He would use parts of it for the United States Constitution too. Madison was still only 25 years old at the time.

George Mason

Later in 1776, Madison became a member of the Virginia House of Delegates. He met Thomas Jefferson there. During the next two years, he looked up to Jefferson and learned a lot from him. They talked a lot about politics and their ideas. They also worked together on things like religious freedom.

Thomas Jefferson

In 1778, Madison was chosen to be on the Governor's Council. This meant that he would be able to give advice to Virginia's first governor, Patrick Henry.

In 1779, Madison became a member of the Continental Congress in Philadelphia, Pennsylvania. He was taking Jefferson's place because Jefferson was moving back to Virginia to be the state's governor. Madison was not yet 30 when he took Jefferson's place. He was one of the youngest people in politics.

Chapter 3: The Father of the Constitution

During Madison's first year in Congress, the Congress made a new type of government. It was called the Articles of Confederation. This gave the states a lot more power than the United States government. Madison did not like the Articles. He thought the colonies needed to work together more. Even though he was young, he liked to talk about the Articles a lot and say he didn't like them. Not enough people would listen.

In 1784, Madison went back to Virginia to be in the House of Delegates again. He helped Thomas Jefferson's "Bill for Religious Liberty." This was like the First Amendment of the Bill of Rights, which gives Americans the right to free speech.

Madison also thought a lot about government. He didn't want common citizens to have too much control of government. This is not how most Americans think anymore, but Madison wanted smart people in charge to know what was right and do it for people. He did not want them to be worried about getting people to vote for them.

By 1787, a lot of other Americans felt the same way Madison did about the Articles of Confederation. America needed a new way to do things. In the summer of 1787, 12 of the 13 states sent men to Philadelphia, Pennsylvania. A lot of these men wanted to come up with changes for the Articles of Confederation, but Madison wanted to write a new Constitution. Madison and Alexander Hamilton wanted to make a whole new government. The meeting would become known as the Constitutional Convention.

Alexander Hamilton

Madison had been studying history to try to find out how to make a new government. He knew more about it than anybody else. The other people at the Constitutional Convention looked up to him, even though he was one of the youngest people there.

Independence Hall in Philadelphia. This is where the Constitutional Convention met.

On May 14, 1787, Madison got to Philadelphia. He already had a plan with him. It was known as the Virginia Plan because the Virginians liked it. Madison showed it to people from other states to try to get them to like it too.

Madison's plan wanted to make a Senate and a House of Representatives. The Senate and House of Representatives would have members from the 13 states. The number of people a state would have in the Senate and the House of Representatives would go by how many people lived in the state. Since Virginia was one of the biggest states, Madison's plan would give Virginia more power.

Madison's plan also wanted the government to have an executive branch with a President and a judicial branch with courts. The courts, Congress, and president would all have some power. This meant nobody would have too much power. Most of the people at the Constitutional Convention liked the idea of having courts, a Congress and a president. But they wanted to change some of the powers that the president and Congress had. Big states, like Virginia, liked the Virginia Plan. It became known as the Big State Plan. Smaller states did not like the plan. They wanted each state to have the same number of people in Congress. This was known as the New Jersey Plan.

Finally, a Connecticut man named Roger Sherman came up with a plan that big states and small states liked. The House of Representatives would have members based on how many people lived in each state. The Senate would have two members from each state.

Roger Sherman was the only person to sign the Declaration of Independence, Articles of Confederation, and the Constitution

On September 17, 1787, the Constitutional Convention agreed on a new Constitution. The

President would be President for 4 years. Senators would be Senators for 6 years. They had to win another election to stay longer. Only the members of the United States Supreme Court would be chosen for life.

Madison voted for the new Constitution. It didn't have everything he wanted, but nobody else got everything they wanted either. Madison was called the Father of the Constitution because they used so much of his plan.

The famous painting *"Scene at the Signing of the Constitution of the United States"*. George Washington is standing at the desk. Benjamin Franklin is sitting in the middle in a blue coat. James Madison is to the right of Franklin. Alexander Hamilton is to the left of Franklin.

Not everyone liked the new Constitution. A lot of Madison's friends in Virginia didn't think it would work. He had to talk to many of them about the Constitution. He wanted other people to like it as much as he did. He also told people that he would make changes to it. He said that he would help write a Bill of Rights that would protect the rights of American citizens. He also told people that most of the future presidents would come from Virginia. He was right about both.

Once Madison talked other Virginians into liking the new Constitution, he worked with people to get other states to accept it. Madison, Alexander Hamilton, and a man named John Jay wrote letters and articles about how great the Constitution was. These letters and articles were called the Federalist Papers. The Federalist Papers are some of the most famous works in American history. People still read them today. They help people know what the Founding Fathers were thinking. Many people think Madison wrote the best Federalist Papers.

John Jay

Madison also wrote the Bill of Rights, even though he was scared that a Bill of Rights would make people argue over the Constitution again. He wrote 20 Amendments to the Constitution. The Bill of Rights would end up being 10 Amendments. He gave the Bill of Rights to Congress in August of 1789. Congress passed it in just a month.

Chapter 4: Early American Government

In 1789, James Madison joined the House of Representatives and was part of the 1st Congress. He wanted to be a Senator, but the people in Virginia's state government didn't pick him. Since he was in the House of Representatives, he had to win people's votes. Madison wanted politicians to do what was best for the country instead of trying to make people happy. But now that he had to win people's votes, his views changed. Madison began to agree more with those who could vote for him.

George Washington was the first President of the United States. He had Alexander Hamilton and Thomas Jefferson helping him. But Hamilton and Jefferson didn't agree on what to do very much. Jefferson and Madison created the Democratic-Republicans. Hamilton and his friends made the Federalists. They were America's first two political parties.

In September of 1794, 43 year old James Madison married a young widow named Dolley Payne Todd. Madison was short and shy, but Dolley was very charming. James and Dolley had a long and happy marriage. Dolley would become one of America's best First Ladies.

Dolley Madison

Madison left Congress in 1797. Washington's vice-president, John Adams, became the second President that year. Madison didn't like Adams very much. Adams was a Federalist. In 1798, the Congress made four laws that said that people could not say bad things about the president or the government. Madison thought that these laws were wrong. He and Jefferson tried to make them go away. They also said that states that did not like those laws did not have to do them.

In the Election of 1800, Thomas Jefferson won. This made Madison happy. Jefferson made Madison his Secretary of State. Madison was part of an important Supreme Court case. President John Adams had made a lot of new judges just before Thomas Jefferson became president. He also tried to make the Supreme Court smaller. This meant Jefferson wouldn't be able to name his own judges.

One of the people Adams made a judge was William Marbury. But Madison and Jefferson wouldn't let him be a judge. Marbury had the Supreme Court decide whether Madison and Jefferson could stop him. The Court ruled for the first time that a law made by Congress and the President was still not legal. They said it was unconstitutional.

Secretary of State Madison tried to keep America out of war. England and France were fighting each other. He and Jefferson also worked hard to get the Louisiana Purchase from France. This made the United States much bigger.

Chapter 5: President Madison

Engraving of President Madison

Madison became the 4th President of the United States in 1808. But even though he won, the people in New England didn't like him. They were still Federalists. Madison's Democratic-Republican Party tried to get some Federalists to like them.

President Madison decided not to trade with France and Great Britain. He didn't want to take sides in their war. But this didn't help America. France and Great Britain did a lot of trade with America. This hurt the economy.

Madison tried to be friendly with Native Americans. He met with some of their chiefs. He wanted Native Americans to be farmers, not hunters. This would let everyone live together. But Americans and Native Americans still fought over land. There were wars with a lot of Native American tribes. To try to beat the Americans, the Native Americans asked the British for help. This scared President Madison. A lot of people in Congress wanted America to go to war with the British.

President Madison didn't know what to do. He asked Congress if America should go to war. It was a close vote. The House voted 79-49 for war. The Senate voted 19-13 for war. People in New England didn't want to go to war at all. All 39 of the Federalists in Congress voted against war. But on June 18, 1812, Madison and Congress decided to go to war. This started the War of 1812.

In 1813, America tried to take Canada but kept losing. The British didn't attack America too much either though. They were fighting the French in Europe. The British weren't worried about America. They had their Navy sail across the Atlantic Ocean to America and shoot at the coast.

In August of 1814, the British attacked Washington D.C. They sent soldiers to burn the city. President Madison had to run away. President Madison wasn't a soldier, but he joined the Army. He had Dolley stay in the White House to try to save stuff before the British came. Dolley got all of President Madison's important papers. She also had a very important picture of George Washington saved. When the British showed up, they burned the White House.

After a few days, the British left Washington D.C. President Madison came back. They needed to rebuild the White House. President Madison started talking to the British about peace. The states in New England were so mad about the war that they were talking about leaving the country. On December 24, 1814, America and Great Britain made peace. The peace treaty didn't change anything though. It just stopped the war.

Without airplanes or railroads, it took a long time for news to reach people. Before some Americans found out about the peace treaty, they fought the British at the Battle of New Orleans. General Andrew Jackson and his American soldiers won the battle. It was the biggest battle of the War of 1812. And it had been fought after the war had ended. The battle made Andrew Jackson a hero. He would later become president.

After the War of 1812, President Madison wanted America to have a bigger army and navy. This would make sure they'd be ready to fight another war better.

Chapter 6: Madison's Last Years

In 1816, James Madisons stopped being president. He was very happy to leave. He didn't like being president anymore. He wanted to retire and live at his nice house, Montpelier.

In 1826, Madison became the president of the University of Virginia. That school had been made by Thomas Jefferson. Madison was president of the school until he died in 1836.

In 1829, Madison helped Virginia make a new constitution for the state. This was the second time he helped write Virginia's constitution. He also wanted to write about the Constitutional Convention of 1787. This would help him make money. Madison needed more money because he had lost a lot of it.

James Madison died in 1836. He was 85 years old. He was the last person who signed the Constitution to die. As the Father of the Constitution, Madison was the last of the Founding Fathers to die.

Alexander Hamilton

Chapter 1: An Orphan

One of America's Founding Fathers wasn't born in the United States. Alexander Hamilton's was born on the island of Nevis on January 12, 1757. Nevis was an island in the West Indies. The West Indies were islands in the Caribbean Sea. The British had them.

Alexander Hamilton's father was James Hamilton. James was born in Scotland and came to the West Indies as a merchant. Alexander's mother, Rachel, was from France.

James Hamilton left Rachel and Alexander in 1766. Alexander was only 9 years old when his dad left him. He and his brother only had their mother. Rachel opened a store on the island of Nevis. She made enough money to let her two boys go to school.

In 1768, Rachel got sick and died. Alexander was only 11 years old. With no parents to take care of them, Alexander and his brother were orphans.

The place where Alexander Hamilton was born.

Alexander Hamilton as a young boy

When he was a teenager, Alexander was a clerk for a company called Beekman and Cruger. The store's owner, Nicholas Cruger, liked Hamilton's work. He liked Alexander so much that he let Alexander run the store on his own for months.

One of the priests on Nevis also liked Hamilton. His name was Hugh Knox. Knox thought Alexander was very smart. He liked that Alexander read a lot of books. Knox and Cruger came up with the idea of sending Hamilton to North America to go to school.

In 1772, Alexander Hamilton sailed to Princeton, New Jersey. He wanted to go to the College of New Jersey, which is called Princeton University today. But Alexander did not go to school much as a child. This meant he had to study hard and go to another school first. In the Fall of 1772, he went to a grammar school in Elizabethtown, New Jersey. He learned the topics that he needed to know so he could go to the College of New Jersey.

Hamilton came to America just before the American Revolution was about to start. He was only 18 years old when it started. Hamilton went to the College of New Jersey but did not like it. He told the school's president that he would only go to school there if he could finish faster. The president said no. Hamilton decided to go to King's College in New York City. That school is now known as Columbia University. Hamilton started going there in 1773.

Statue of Alexander Hamilton at Hamilton Hall. The statue is part of Columbia

University.

Hamilton loved living in New York City. It was very different than his home in the West Indies. Hamilton was now in a big city. New York was one of the biggest cities in the 13 colonies. Hamilton felt like New York City was full of money and power.

Hamilton also liked to read about politics. He came to New York when the colonists were mad at the British. The Coercive Acts were a bunch of laws passed by the British Parliament in 1774. Parliament made these laws because of the Boston Tea Party on December 16, 1773. The colonists got even madder at Parliament. 56 men went to Philadelphia in 1774 to talk about the Coercive Acts. The meeting was called the First Continental Congress. They wanted King George III to treat them better.

In 1774 and 1775, Alexander Hamilton wrote about the First Continental Congress. He was also mad at the British. He liked what the First Continental Congress did. Hamilton wanted to fight the British, but he was still nice to people who liked the British too.

Chapter 2: The Revolutionary War

Like many men his age, Alexander Hamilton wanted to fight in the Revolutionary War. He joined one of New York City's militias. A militia was a group of men who learned how to fire guns and act like an army. They were very important for the colonies. They were most of the soldiers fighting the British.

Hamilton was a very good soldier. In 1776, Hamilton joined George Washington's army. Washington's army had come to New York to fight the British for New York City.

George Washington

    The British won the battle for New York City. This made Washington and his army march to New Jersey. The British chased them all the way into Pennsylvania. Things weren't going well for the Americans.

    On Christmas Day of 1776, the Americans finally won a big battle. They beat the British at the Battle of Trenton. They were able to do this because George Washington played a trick on the British. He had his men row across the Delaware River at night. The British did not think he would do this, so they were surprised. The British had hired German soldiers to help them fight. These soldiers were called Hessians. The Hessians celebrated and got drunk. They weren't ready to fight at Trenton.

A famous painting of Washington crossing the Delaware River.

Hamilton helped Washington fight in the Battle of Trenton. Washington thought Hamilton did a good job. He asked Hamilton to be one of his personal helpers. In March 1777, Hamilton became Washington's aide-de-camp. That meant he talked to Washington all the time and helped Washington do all kinds of things. Hamilton grew up speaking French with his mother. That meant that he could work with the French people that Washington was trying to get to help the Americans. This was great for Washington. Washington had one French soldier known as the Marquis de Lafayette. Lafayette was such a good soldier during the Revolutionary War that America made him an American citizen even though he was French!

Illustration of Washington and the Marquis de Lafayette

   Hamilton also talked to Americans to try to get more men to join the army. This helped him learn about Americans. One thing he learned was that people really cared about what state they came from. Their state was more important to them than being part of the United States. This meant that they might not take orders from someone who was from another state.

   Hamilton didn't like this. The war was going to end soon, and he wanted the United States to do well. Hamilton wanted people to love their country more than their state.

   Washington and Hamilton also began to argue as the war was ending. Hamilton wanted to fight as a soldier, but Washington wanted him to stay and be his personal helper. Washington let him be a soldier again, but the two stopped being friends for a long time.

   When the Revolutionary War was over, a lot of people liked Hamilton. They also knew he was very smart. In 1782, the people of New York chose him to be in the Continental Congress. When he got there, Hamilton found out that the colonies didn't like to work together. America was trying to make a peace treaty with Britain and France, but the colonies could not agree on what the treaty should say.

One of the problems was that the country did not have a Constitution yet. They only had what was called the Articles of Confederation. This gave the states a lot more power than the United States government. Hamilton kept telling people that they had to agree to work together. Not enough people would listen.

Hamilton was tired of working in Congress. He wanted to do something else, so he became a lawyer. He found a type of law that he was good at. He started helping men who had stayed loyal to the British during the war. Americans had attacked them and taken their property. Hamilton helped them get a fair trial.

Chapter 3: The Constitution

Even though he was no longer in the Continental Congress, Hamilton kept working to try to make people see that America was in trouble. A few men who agreed with him said he could write letters to the leaders of the other states. These letters would give the reason why the Articles of Confederation were not working.

By 1787, a lot of other Americans felt the same way Hamilton did. America needed a new way to do things. In the summer of 1787, 12 of the 13 states sent men to Philadelphia, Pennsylvania. A lot of these men wanted to come up with changes for the Articles of Confederation, but Hamilton wanted to write a new Constitution. Hamilton and James Madison wanted to make a whole new government. The meeting would become known as the Constitutional Convention.

James Madison

Hamilton was one of New York's people at the Constitutional Convention. He wanted big changes, but the other men from New York wanted a small and weak government. Hamilton also hadn't gone to school as much as most of the other people at the Convention. He felt like they were smarter than him. Some of them, like James Madison, had studied different governments. Hamilton had never read a book about it.

Hamilton wanted America's government to be bigger and stronger. This scared a lot of people. They felt Hamilton wanted government to be too much like the British. That was the one they had just fought a war to get away from. Hamilton wanted the president to be president for life. People thought that would the president be like a king. Hamilton also wanted Senators to serve for life. This would make them like the members of the House of Lords in British Parliament.

On September 17, 1787, the Constitutional Convention agreed on a new Constitution. The President would be President for 4 years. Senators would be Senators for 6 years. They had to win another election to stay longer. Only the members of the United States Supreme Court would be chosen for life.

The famous painting *"Scene at the Signing of the Constitution of the United States"*. George Washington is standing up at the desk. Benjamin Franklin is sitting in the center in a blue shirt. Alexander Hamilton is sitting to the left of Franklin. James Madison is sitting to the right of Franklin.

   Hamilton voted for the new Constitution. It didn't have everything he wanted, but nobody else got everything they wanted either. Hamilton helped talk people into liking the new Constitution. He, James Madison and a man named John Jay wrote letters and articles about how good the Constitution was. These letters and articles were called the Federalist Papers. The Federalist Papers are some of the most famous works in American history. People still read them today. They help people know what the Founding Fathers were thinking.

John Jay

Hamilton wrote most of the Federalist Papers. He talked a lot about the role of the new Supreme Court. He wanted everyone to know about how good it would be for Americans to have Supreme Court judges rule on laws.

Chapter 4: Secretary of the Treasury

By 1789, Washington and Hamilton were friends again. Washington was America's first president. He asked Hamilton to be his Secretary of the Treasury. Hamilton was happy to be working in New York City. New York City was America's capitol city. Washington D.C. had not been built yet.

Washington picked Thomas Jefferson to be his Secretary of State. Jefferson knew a lot about Europe. This made him a good person to be Secretary of State. But Jefferson and Hamilton disagreed a lot on politics. Jefferson wanted a smaller government and stronger states. Hamilton wanted a bigger government and weaker states.

Thomas Jefferson

When Washington became president, the United States was still weak. They had fought the Revolutionary War a few years earlier. During the war, the states owed a lot of money. They had borrowed money from other countries to spend on the war. Hamilton had an idea. In January of 1790, Hamilton wrote the First Report on the Public Credit and gave it to Congress. He said that the United States government should take the states' debts and pay them off. Jefferson did not like the idea. He thought it would give the United States government too much power over states. He and Hamilton worked on the Compromise of 1790, which gave some states extra land for paying the money they owed.

Hamilton also wanted to make a National Bank. It would be owned by the United States government but run by regular people. Hamilton thought it would make the American economy stronger. The bank would be able to make money and loan money to businesses. Jefferson did not like the idea. He thought it would not be good for the country's farmers. Washington listened to both Hamilton and Jefferson. He took Hamilton's side.

In 1791, Hamilton came up with a grand plan for the American economy. His Report on Manufactures to Congress was the name of the plan. Most Americans did not like his idea. They worked on farms and sided with Jefferson. Hamilton argued that factories would help America be richer and stronger. It would lead to better machines and help people not have to work so hard. This meant that people could do more with less.

Hamilton also thought new businesses would bring more people to the country. This would give the new nation more workers. It would also help America get more people to pay taxes. He wanted to give businesses from Europe money if they would move to America. He also wanted to make it easier for people to invent new things that the country could use.

Jefferson did not like it that Washington took Hamilton's side so much. Jefferson started talking to people who agreed with him, like James Madison and Aaron Burr. They decided to work together. They made a political party called the Democratic-Republicans. They wanted to fight against Hamilton's ideas.

Hamilton decided to start his own political party. They were called the Federalists. The two parties soon started arguing with each other. They often wrote bad things about the other side in newspapers.

Hamilton's last job as Secretary of the Treasury was to work with Great Britain. Washington sent John Jay to England to make a treaty. He had Hamilton tell Jay what he was to do. Hamilton's main goal was make sure America and Great Britain could trade with each other. He also didn't want them to go to war. This would help America's economy grow.

The treaty was called the Jay Treaty after John Jay. Jefferson didn't like it. He said that it made the United States a slave to Great Britain. He and his friends liked France more than Great Britain. But Hamilton wrote articles about why people should vote for it. In 1795, Hamilton again got his way.

Chapter 5: A New Job

Hamilton quit being the Secretary of the Treasury in 1795. Washington was done being president in 1796. Washington left with a Farewell Address. He wrote the speech with the help of Hamilton. In the speech, Washington gave Americans some good advice. He said three important things in his final address. First, he told Americans they should stay out of wars fought in Europe. Second, he asked Americans not to fight with each other. Finally, he talked about how important it was for people to live good lives and do the right thing.

Hamilton didn't like to talk about his part in writing Washington's Farewell Address. The Democratic-Republicans knew he had helped write the speech though. They didn't like Hamilton, but they did like Washington. Since they liked Washington, they didn't talk about Hamilton.

Washington's vice president, John Adams, became the next president. Hamilton wasn't in the government while Adams was president. But John Adams was a Federalist like Hamilton. Hamilton talked with Adams sometimes.

In 1798, France and America almost went to war. France wouldn't let American ships sail to

England. This was hurting the American economy. Congress told the United States Navy to attack French ships. Washington and Hamilton also wanted to fight the French. The United States had not really declared war on France, but they were fighting French ships.

John Adams had not fought in the Revolutionary War. He was only a lawyer. Adams needed a general with military experience. His first choice was George Washington. Washington didn't want to leave home though. John Adams picked Alexander Hamilton. Hamilton got money from Congress and made an army. He also came up with some plans, but they weren't used. The fighting ended in 1800. The French never fought in America.

Americans were unhappy with President Adams. This meant that Thomas Jefferson or one of his friends would probably be the next president. Hamilton also didn't like Adams anymore. He thought Adams wasn't good enough with people. In the Election of 1800, Hamilton tried to help another Federalist named Charles Cotesworth Pinckney win.

In the Election of 1800, the Democratic-Republicans wanted Thomas Jefferson to be president and Aaron Burr to be vice president. They beat John Adams, but the Democratic-Republicans made a mistake. They gave Burr as many votes as Jefferson. This meant the House of Representatives had to pick the president. The Federalists still were in control of the House of Representatives.

A lot of Federalists didn't like Jefferson, so they wanted to make Burr president. But Hamilton didn't like Burr at all. They had been enemies as far back as 1791. That was when Burr beat Hamilton's father-in-law for a Senate seat. He decided to back Thomas Jefferson instead. He told one man, "Nothing has given me so much chagrin as the intelligence that the Federal party were thinking seriously of supporting Mr. Burr for president. I should consider the execution of the plan as [hurting] the country and signing their own death warrant. Mr. Burr will probably make [promises], but he will laugh in his sleeve while he makes them and will break them the first moment it may serve his purpose."

Hamilton didn't like the things Jefferson did. But he thought that a man who stood for something was better than one who stood for nothing. He got those who agreed with him to vote for Jefferson. Hamilton had so much power that he was seen as choosing the president himself. This made Burr very mad at Hamilton.

Aaron Burr

With Hamilton's help, Jefferson became the third president. He was taking power away from Hamilton's own political party. This is one of the first times in history that a government handed over control to its political opponents without a fight. The Federalists never again had a president. The Federalists would be gone by 1820.

Chapter 6: The Hamilton-Burr Duel

Alexander Hamilton monument near the site of his duel with Aaron Burr

Aaron Burr wanted to be president. When Hamilton went against him, Burr was very mad. The two men continued to fight with each other in the next few years. Burr wanted to be Governor of New York in 1804. He was running as a Democratic-Republican, but some Federalists also liked him. Hamilton tried to do everything he could to make sure Burr lost his election in 1804.

When Burr lost the race, he was even madder at Hamilton. Some newspapers in New York said that Hamilton had told his friends Burr was dangerous and evil. Burr told Hamilton that he wanted an apology, but Hamilton wouldn't. He thought Burr was a bad man. Burr never got the apology he wanted, so he challenged Hamilton to a duel. Hamilton accepted it. The duel was set for July 11th, 1804.

Illustration of the Hamilton-Burr duel

Hamilton and Burr had both been in duels before, but Hamilton had never fired a shot during any of them. Hamilton's own son, Philip, had been killed in a duel in 1801. . A lot of people didn't like duels. Some states made duels illegal. New York was one of those states. This meant Hamilton and Burr would have to duel in New Jersey.

On the morning of July 11, 1804, the two men and their best friends rowed across the Hudson River to New Jersey. Even today, nobody knows for sure what happened at the duel. The people who were there said different things about the duel.

Only a few facts are known for sure. Two shots were fired during the duel, one by Hamilton and one by Burr. No one knows who fired the first shot. Hamilton's shot missed so badly that it hit a branch above Burr. This probably meant that Hamilton did not want to hit Burr with his shot. He probably thought Burr would try to miss him too. In most duels, the men would not try to kill each other.

The pistols used in the duel

Hamilton's shot wasn't close to Burr, but Burr's shot hit Hamilton in the chest. Hamilton was hurt very badly. He could not move. He knew he was going to die. After the duel, Hamilton was brought back to a friend's home in New York. He lay in bed while his friends and family visited him. He died the next day. He was only 49 years old. He was buried in New York City.

The duel made Americans very angry. When Hamilton died, people were mad at Burr. They thought it meant Burr had meant to kill him. Most people thought duels should not be used for revenge. Burr was arrested for murder in both New Jersey and New York. But he was never tried for a crime. People were so mad at him that his political career was over.

It's believed Hamilton lay against this rock after being shot

A portrait of Hamilton. It was used for the $10 bill

Made in the USA
Columbia, SC
19 April 2020